To my parents, Haider and Tahira.

Haider Faizullah

MY SAGE

Translated by: Mohamed Haider

AUSTIN MACAULEY PUBLISHERS™
LONDON • CAMBRIDGE • NEW YORK • SHARJAH

Copyright © Haider Faizullah 2022
Translated by Mohamed Haider

The right of Haider Faizullah and Mohamed Haider to be identified as author and translator of this work has been asserted by them in accordance with section 77 and 78 of the Copyright, Designs and Patents Act 1988.

All rights reserved. No part of this publication may be reproduced, stored in a retrieval system, or transmitted in any form or by any means, electronic, mechanical, photocopying, recording, or otherwise, without the prior permission of the publishers.

Any person who commits any unauthorised act in relation to this publication may be liable to criminal prosecution and civil claims for damages.

The story, the experiences, and the words are the author's alone.

A CIP catalogue record for this title is available from the British Library.

ISBN 9781398486263 (Paperback)
ISBN 9781398486270 (ePub e-book)

www.austinmacauley.com

First Published 2022
Austin Macauley Publishers Ltd®
1 Canada Square
Canary Wharf
London
E14 5AA

Table of Contents

Foreword (By the Translator)	7
A Prologue of Love	9
My Story with Him	14
The First Meeting	17
Alms Relieve Fever	23
Sheikh Eid Jareer	27
The Celebrations Hall	*28*
As-Sheikh Abd-Alraoaf Awadi	32
I Couldn't Sleep	35
Leave Your ICU Bed	39
From Where Did You Receive This?	44
Weed Was Aspirin	48
Diabetic Coma	54
The Orphans' Painting	57
A Message from the Deceased	60
Sheikh X	66
The Garbage Carrier	69

My Sage's Spouse	71
Al Qahhawi	73
Do You Think That I Don't See?	77
The Migraine Is Gone	79
Haj Abdulraoof Sharaf or the Pilgrimage	81
Mr. Hamid and the Infliction of Marsafa	90
My Sage's Letter	*93*
Drink from Me (Poem)	97
About Him	98

Foreword
(By the Translator)

My father had a sage. He was a pole; the target that would take you to the Lord. His presence as my father's sage changed the course of our life. A sage is a guardian to the Lord and a scholar or a sheikh is a translator of the judicial religious laws to the public, but he did it all, hence I would like to refer to him as 'master.'

In early 2000s, and during our stay in Egypt, an Iraqi man married to an Alexandrian Egyptian lady was visiting my father's sage. He took the train from Alexandria to Tanta where the sage lived. The train had a stop in the central station in Tanta passing by a small level crossing right in front of the sage's house. The house is a small-sized building in front of a two-lane crossing. On his train ride, the Iraqi man directed his thoughts to the sage. As he was traveling in a multiple cabinets train, he thought, *why do I have to travel to the station, take a cab and return back to the sage's house; what if the train stopped in front of the building?* It was a passing thought that soon became a reality as the train slowed down early, stopping stationary while placing his cabinet door right at the level crossing. He departed the train with his luggage and the train continued its journey normally to the station and everything looked routine. Was it a silent miracle, I wonder? In our everyday lives we encounter extraordinary events that we fail to observe or we translate these events with our pre-acquired knowledge. It is very easy to believe in a miracle you are raised knowing it had occurred, although the evidence of Jesus walking on water was always the information received from trusted acquaintances, it is now believed by millions; yet a modern-day extraordinary event is harder to believe as there is always a preferable translation in our minds. My father in his book writes short stories that he had lived through or he came to know directly from those who lived through the events. I believe that my role as a translator compels me to be as literal as possible in translating the context of my father's book to the reader.

A Prologue of Love

Rumi says:

"When the spirit of a lover breathes upon this world, it sets it on fire."

This is a meaning for what comes after and follows the messages of God's prophets. A lantern of light is still shining brightly upon the world today, it is the guidance from the spirit of the Prophet Mohammed that is flowing through different parts of the world and bringing clairvoyance to those who can see the beauty of this light. This light is described by the Lord as the niche where there is a lamp that is in a glass looking like a brilliant star which was lit from a blessed tree. This is the light and guidance of Allah – exalted and blessed – which dwells in the heart of the believing human to illuminate the world.

The beloved Prophet Mohammed did breathe upon this world with his sanctified breaths; those breaths that had the complete love and passion to his love and desire; Allah. His heart's attachment to Allah made everything else easy.

The light of the Lord that shone on the world from the glorified spirit of the prophet is a light of clairvoyance that is not seen by the eyes. This light was not observed by all those who physically witnessed the prophet, but rather to those who were willing and competent to accept this light and its guidance. This light is not seen by the eyes but is rather like the photons of light; the photons are not seen by the eyes but are observed by seeing other matter.

Amr Hisham Al Makhzoomi did see the prophet but became his enemy and was named "Abu Jahal – of Ignorance." On the other hand, the prophet's cousin, Ali son of Abu Taleb, saw the prophet and became the gate to the prophet as the prophet is the City of knowledge and Ali is its gate (this is a well-known saying by the prophet).

I would like to reflect here on the meeting of Jalal al Din Al Rumi with Shams Tabrez. Shams was to the public a simple man in rags and dishdasha, but to Rumi he was a Sun. He found in Shams a heart where the light of the Lord dwelled. He found in him the clairvoyance that he needed to shine and to pronounce all the lyrics and poems he had written. Those words are today a reminder to the oblivious and a flowing river of poetry for the lovers to drink from. These words ignite the love in the heart to its ultimate beloved the Creator, Allah, in those seeking pureness in their souls and those pursuing a path to the truth that emerges when the heart is clear from everything other than Allah.

I would like to remind my reader of Allah's holy saying, "My heavens and my earths are not wide enough for me, but the heart of my believing slave is."

There are always, in every time, those with a heart for the Lord and as He says in his holy book, "Then Allah will bring a people whom He loves and they love Him," (ALMAEDA:54). And maybe you won't see them, and most people won't see them. Even if their light was as a bright as that of the sun, it is in another layer of existence and is not seen by the eyes but by clairvoyance.

Beware that sparks of this light will appear and will be identified. Yet only the true heart will follow its guidance and will not deny observing it. Some will deny as they will fail to comprehend even if they managed to see the spark.

In my book, my dear reader, I am reflecting on some of the sparks of this light. I hope these real stories speak to you and remind you of how far you are from the field. Many heroes and characters of my stories are living as I write this book. Remember, we humans are truly loved by our Creator.

My sage or master Mohamed Ismail El Laithy was an illuminated lantern in this era. If you went to him with a request, he fulfilled it; if you went to him for knowledge, he taught you; if you went to him for guidance, he gave it to you; if you went to him with love, he would give you more. My master was a spark clearly observed by whoever had an open eye, he was a guidance to one's behaviors and progress.

"Every vein in this young man beats for Allah," is how Sheikh Eid Jareer described my master in my master's youth. Sheikh Jareer was a man of clairvoyance. A friend of mine and a companion of my master once described to me his relationship with our master; he said, "When I first met our master, I was in my early twenties. I had then become a follower of his and I was under the impression that he was older than me by roughly 10 years. I came later to know that he was younger than me when I had taken his passport for completing traveling arrangements. I then knew that he had a majesty that was not related to his age." This friend of mine is Mohamed Al Abd lilah, he passed away; may the Lord be merciful on his soul. I met him in his eighties roughly.

I do not intend to summarize my master's life through this book. I want to share some stories through which I hope to stir the winds of love in the heart of my reader. I hope this love will glow your heart with love that can burn everything other than Allah so that the heart remains pure only to Him and thereby I will be granted the intercession of anyone who will be influenced and will receive the Lord's clairvoyance.

When I initially started writing these stories, I intended for them to be distributed after my death so it will not be directed toward me. However, when I settled, I found in myself only His presence so I found no reason to wait. I then wrote this introduction and I do not know whether I will be leaving this world soon or whether my master has intended for these stories to be distributed in my life.

The time I spent with him was merely a short duration of twenty years. He had passed away 14 years ago and since he has gone, every breath is heavier, and every minute is longer. It feels to me as if I had lost him only yesterday. My dear reader, you might find me in confusion but know that when I was with him, days flew without me feeling and my status with him is never ending. My master was a light of Allah and Allah's light is always shining.

I had written a poem describing my feelings (the original poem is in Arabic and this is a translation of the poetry):

    O singer, be kind
    As my heart panteths to him
    O singer, don't whine
    For I smell traits of him
    O reciter, don't remind
    For I am an orphan of him

They say you are consumed
In the memory of him
I say I am in doom
As I wait for meeting him
His date is my end
So my tears fall and wend
And when my heart did taste his presence
The time denied it
And when he did embrace me
He dictated that I be at a distance.

My friends reproached me on the ending of my poem where I say he dictated that I be at a distance. However, I yearn for him and my soul feels him. This life to me is a barrier between seeing his bright face for he is to me like the sun in midday when it is hidden by the clouds as the children chant "Bright sun, shine down on me…"

My Story with Him

On the day I opened my eyes
I found his yearn knocking my door
His name was ringing in my sides
With love it filled me in my core
His name came out in sunrise
And in my heart it did more
Enclosed my senses with its light
proclaimed my status with its might.

I then got lost in his love
I found my passion
I then knew he is the one
In A L and I his mission
In her womb it all got mixed
Along my flesh and my bones
And when I knew what got fixed
I learned the Lord me has picked
I then had lost all but him
I did not know what he did
Evident became my loss in him
And love had shown what he did
And then my parts I began to veil

While he praised and cleared my ail.

Lo, will I see him?
No, he is afar of sight
Master of soil he is?
Yes, we are sands from casts
Eons of time are between us
Yes, time a barrier hast
In desertion I shall remain to be
From him, patience I might have had.

Will I get to see a date with them
Will I get to have a state from them
Will I get to feel forgiveness of them
And then I heard a call from them
O my family, I did call
On a bush of flames, I did fall
A lantern of light, I might obtain
And in its rays, we can fain.

He loaned me his corner
A new life in my core and ore
Lo, in him I was a martyr
And I called back once more
the lamp I foresaw I do hold.

I came back hailing
I have found my calling
The lantern is shining
With rays that are guiding
Ali is the eternal light

He shone in my sky bright
to him I was enslaved in kind
Come and see my guiding light
O tribe of mine and walk its side
You are a fool, they said,
And who is he? They stressed,
A teacher, scholar, or a sage
They expressed,
His beauty I did see
And Ali I found as he.

The First Meeting

My master (may his soul be sanctified by Allah) said, "Meetings are timed appointments," as he told us the story of a righteous man who came to Cairo (in the sixties of the last century) where he met a young boy walking with his parents in Cairo's airport. The man rushed toward the young boy with glee and hugged him with happiness, announcing loudly "This is my boy…this is my boy."

The European parents assumed he was a freak who wanted to kidnap their child; they attempted to release him but the man held his embrace.

He was about to be arrested when he regained his stance; he smiled to the parents and explained, "This boy was standing beside me in the 'am I not' world – a pre-existence world where God asked 'Am I not your Lord?' – and I poked this boy to say yes and my finger went into his chest from the right side." (A group of people had to translate to the European family.)

The family was skeptical and they wanted the man to be arrested, he asked them to open the boy's shirt and he showed them the place where he was able to insert his finger on the right side of the boy's chest with no bones restricting his finger.

The European family became curious to learn about the world of 'Am I not?' and the man explained to them what the Quran says about this 'pre-earth' world were God asked mankind to testify for him with lordship. The family turned to Islam after this event.

This life is a bridge between a life before and a life after. We came to know through our prophet's sayings and the real experiences of individuals that spirits are enlisted soldiers, if they identify each other, they are more familiar and friendly to one another.

In this life we experience events that alter our status, programs, and directions. It has been told by Abu Taleb Az Zahdi Al Jylani and many others that Imam Ali said, "I came to identify Allah as He repeals determinations and revokes mettles, whenever I started/had the mettle for a matter He came in between me and my mettle, and whenever I was determined, he revoked the destiny in my determination, hence, I knew that the manger is Allah."

Praised and exalted He is. He acts as He wants and puts in destiny what He wills and all what is in His destiny is of wisdom and benevolence to His slaves.

My first meeting with my master was in my homeland Oman toward the end of 1984. I had then been recently back from 'Hawza,' the blessed educational school of Islamic religious studies in Iran. I had returned with an intention to get married and return back to Iran to continue in 'Hawza.'

On those days; being a single person in Hawza was difficult especially on students from countries that do not have communities from their homelands in Iran. Building a stable life was difficult.

Thanks to Allah I had managed to find a partner in my life. She had accepted to accompany me in my journey, acknowledging the difficulties and challenges expected to be faced especially as students in Iran faced a harsh lifestyle in those days.

We started planning to move to Iran for me to continue my studies and scholarship when I heard that a high mystical scholar from Egypt was visiting Muscat and would be staying at a house of a family friend. My father (May Allah bestow on him with His Mercy) used to engage me and my brothers in our childhood with tales about Shams Tabrez and his relationship with Jalal Al Din. He used to tell us about my Uncle Mohammed and his relationship with 'Al Mirza' – Ali Al Qathi Al Tabatabai – through Sayyid Hassan Al Moasawi. My father used to speak highly of Sayyid Hassan and used to share with us his experience with reciting the prayers and *thikr* rituals instructed to him from 'Al Mirza.'

My father once told me that he had received an Omani cap from his brother Mohammed which had 'There is no God but Allah' stitched on it. My uncle passed it on to my father as he migrated to India during the second world war and my father used to wear the cap sitting on a bed on the roof. He used to experience as if he was rising with the bed above the ground as he recited the name of Allah as per the instructions he had received to recite.

My father had a heart filled with love for Imam Ali and a lot of attachment to him. He used to teach us that the gate and path to Allah's knowledge and wisdom is through Ali. Ali is a flowing river in the world and all those who are close to Allah are drinking from this river and they are attached to Allah through this path. He used to explain to us that to reach to Allah, you have to find a sage which will take you to Imam Ali while reminding us of a popular saying by Imam Ali, "Perished is a person who doesn't have a wise sage who guides them."

My dear reader, I want you to feel me in the moment when I heard that "a sage from Egypt is visiting Oman and there is a dinner at the house of…" I was then a student in the religious school of Hawza and I was the son who learned from his father that the path to the Lord is through a sage. I became overwhelmed with anticipation to meet this man to join the path of the Lord, the path that the mighty prophet started and was inherited by the most excellent student Imam Ali who was the soul of the prophet as the Quran states, "If someone argues with you over this after the knowledge that has come to you say, 'come, let us call our sons and your sons, our women and your women, ourselves and yourselves then pray and revoke the curse of Allah upon the liars," (AL IMRAN: 61).

I went to the dinner – which I was not invited to – along with my elder brother Irshad. The gathering was filled with elder men who were from my father's age group. The host – who was a family friend – introduced me to my master by saying, "This is our boy Haider."

My master replied, "Do not say 'our boy Haider' but say, 'Sayyid Haider.'"

The host replied, "I did not intend to derogate him but he is like a son to me."

My master replied, "Yes, I am aware," and then he looked at me and I still can remember his eyes from thirty years ago.

On the following evening the same family friend hosted a gathering in his farmhouse, 100 km from Muscat. Myself and my brother joined the gathering. There was a heavy rain in the evening and the host remembered that he had kept sacks of dry cement outdoors without covering them. He left the gathering and came back later and explained, "Everything was wet from the rain except the cement sacks, praise to Allah, they were dry and I covered them." This event was engraved in my memory and I believed that the cement was saved by the blessed presence of my master.

My master decided to return back to Muscat along with me and my brother. On our drive back the valleys and roads had been flooded. Many of the other guests had difficulties making the road back but we were not stopped by any flooded road. During the ride I told him of my intention to join him and become his disciple and he replied to me with a story of a man who was looking for a sage and every sage he went to gave him a miraculous sign and whenever he identified it, he left the sage and moved on. When this man was asked why did he do so, he replied, "I am looking for the one who will guide me to Allah, not to himself," and then my master continued, "O my son, your sage is not the one who conducts the miracle for you but the one who makes it happen through you."

My master reminded me of the teaching of Imam Jaafar al Saadiq to a man who asked him, "Who is the Imam in my era?"

Imam Jaafar taught him a prayer to read, "Elohim, let me know You because if I don't know You, I will not know my prophet. Elohim, let me know my prophet because if I don't know my prophet, I will not know Your representative/argument. Elohim, let me know Your representative/argument because if I didn't know Your representative, I will be lost from my faith."

On that day, I decided not to return to Hawza – religious scholarship school – but to join my master who was the Lord's light, who Allah gave me the luck of meeting.

Alms Relieve Fever

I am sharing here a story I had heard directly from my master while he was preaching on the reliance on Allah. Many people claim that they trust and rely on Allah, but this cannot be observed in their actions. Surely, Allah, blessed and exalted be He, has the most exalted attributes. People are in different levels in their reliance on Allah. Some people speak of their reliance on God and they would praise any conversation or speech in this subject, however, their selves are inattentive to this and their reliance is to what they are used to from causes and reasons. Others do believe within themselves in reliance on Allah and they revert to the reasons while avoiding entrust (which is false reliance on Allah without putting any effort from oneself), this is while they are aware that the reasons forsaken are not what they are reliant on, but are forsaken out of worship to the Lord as they follow the reasons through His laws and norms in nature and out of abidance to Him. You will identify in these people wisdom and reason and you will not find them prone to emotional inclinations and desires. There are many levels and stages between the groups we have defined and the first level up is what is titled by the righteous as a move from a 'hidden polytheism' to a 'hidden hypocrisy' whereas the final level is 'complete monotheism'.

A person who doesn't follow the reasons in life as they are relying on the creator of all reasons, Allah, they have transgressed against God, blessed be He. While a person who is fully reliant on the reasons in life without Allah, the creator of all reasons, this person has placed independent potency in these reasons and has fallen into 'hidden polytheism/blasphemy'. It is Allah who has given reasons their causes. Additionally, whoever perceives that the actions and activities can only be accomplished through their reasons, even if this person believes in Allah being the ultimate reason-creator, they then have put a limit to Allah's potency and a weakness in His monarchy and this is a 'hidden infidelity'. To be pure, you should perceive that the only real doer is Allah, exalted be He, and all the reasons are His norms and laws that He did place with outcomes and with causes. You should also perceive that the abilities in these reasons are only existent or running in them by the Will of Allah, and hence, all abilities are in the hand of Allah, and you are required to seek the outcomes through these reasons as a manner through which you are extolling Him and obeying Him through following His natural norms, otherwise, all your trust and reliance is to Him as you are not to perceive any other doer but Him. It is indeed the case that all your efforts in acquiring the reasons is through His potency and His will, as you do not have any will nor any potency other than in an external form which is merely a branch of your extolling and praise and obedience to Him, blessed and exalted be He, whether you identified this or not. Blessed and exalted be He says in Quran: "All the seven skies and the earth and all those therein extol/praise for Him, and there not a single thing that does not extol by His thanks, but you do not understand their extolling/praise, surely He is Forbearing, Most-Forgiving".

Allah has placed norms, laws, reasons and their causes, and it is in His hand when they are active or not, and Allah does as He wants whichever way He wants. You can see in life how prayers cure the ill and pleads clear pains. You would have also heard of what Allah granted His prophets from miracles as He made the staff of Moses part the sea and made a call from His servant raise the dead. He remains omnipotent and nothing can stop His will for all the reign is for Him, praised and blessed be He.

The sayyed – my master – describes that during his youth, on a day, he had left to attend a gathering – majlis of worship and remembrance of Allah and saleh on His prophet (peace be upon him and his family). It was a long gathering and he arrived home late at night. As he arrived home, he found his wife holding one of their children with a very high fever and the baby was trembling from the heat. His wife requested that he should immediately get a physician to visit the home to check on the baby. He left the home and started walking in small steps as if he wanted to remain short from reaching the physician. He was in turmoil as on one hand his baby was feverish, and his wife was waiting for him to get a doctor as she stood helpless back home. On the other hand, he was going in the middle of the night to wake-up the doctor and bring him home while he had few money-changes in his pocket that would not be near to the physician's charges. While his thoughts floated, he remembered the saying of the prophet "remediate your sick persons with alms". He then figured where he should go. His steps quickened to compensate for any delays from this earlier walk until he reached the place and emptied his pockets. He was then content that he had done the required reasons in this life for seeking remedy and he headed home.

When he arrived home, it was quiet and calm. The fever was gone from the boy and he was healthy. His wife was waiting for him, but she didn't enquire about the doctor and the whole house was in peace.

Sheikh Eid Jareer

In 1993, I traveled to Egypt to spend few days alongside my master, Mohamed Ismail Al Laithy An Nimr. My traveling days fell on the month of 'Shaaban.' 'Shaaban' is a month with great weight and significance in the Islamic calendar. The Islamic calendar is a lunar calendar upon which all main Islamic celebrations are dated and celebrated.

On the second day of Shabaan, I had arrived to Tanta and was sitting in my master's daily gathering in his library on the first floor of his building which we refer to as the 'Hall of Ahabab Al Safa.' Every night, my sage would come down from his apartment on the second floor to his library on the first floor to meet and greet his visitors and some of his followers that attended to listen to him daily.

On that night, preparations were being made for the birthday of Imam Hussain's celebrations to be conducted on the following day.

In Egypt there are two annular celebrations for Imam Hussain's birthday; a popular one and an actual one.

The popular celebration is held on a five-day period with an attendance that reached to 5 million attendees according to some polls. This celebration is conducted on a date that corresponds to the date the holy head of Imam Hussain arrived in Egypt, as mentioned in some historical references accepted by Egyptian historians.

The other celebration is on the third day of Shaaban which corresponds to the actual birthday. In Egypt, the actual birthday celebrations are limited and are only conducted by some of the Sufi/mystical groups.

Most of my master's disciples were noting any instructions from my master for final preparations for the celebrations from inviting munshids (artists), sheikhs, and other arrangements. Before my master left his library chamber, which we were gathered in, he turned toward me and said, "My son, tomorrow a person who loves you dearly will come, you will meet him if Allah permits but you haven't seen him before." He then left the library and headed back to his quarters without explaining to me how or when I will meet him, nor how he looked, or his name. I told myself that tomorrow was near coming and I would soon know what he intended if Allah wills.

On the following day, I had planned to visit Cairo during daytime with a plan to arrive back to Tanta prior to the start of the celebrations. However, due to unforeseen circumstances my return got delayed. By the time I arrived, my master had started the celebration as he led the event from his chair at the heart of the hall; guests had arrived, and the venue was mostly occupied.

The Celebrations Hall

My master had a building where he accommodated his children and held his sermons. As you would enter the building, a long set of stairs would face you and a corridor to the left. The corridor would end in a junction where you would head left passing by the praying hall to reach to the celebration's venue. You would enter the venue from its end and furthest to the right was where my master was always seated at the heart of the hall.

At the junction you could head straight and enter an Arabic sitting arrangement. The main celebrations hall would be to your left and my master would be seated to your left.

As I previously mentioned, I arrived in Tanta after the event had started and the venue was filled with guests and visitors; I entered through the Arabic sitting room.

As I entered the Arabic sitting room, I searched for a seat at the corners of the room but none were available. I headed toward the edge of the Arabic sitting room to sit in view of the celebration's venue on the floor. I was dressed in pants and a shirt; my attire was similar to the attire of other guests. I scanned the hall and my eyes fell on a man sitting against the wall in line with our sage. He looked at me and made space for me and gestured to me to sit next to him.

I realized that he was the same person my master had told me about, and I don't know how this understanding fell to me, it felt as if I knew him and loved him dearly. Later I came to know he was Sheikh Ali Khalaf from a village in northern Sina close to Gaza's borders with Egypt. How he came to know me and I came to know him is a mystery that I dare say I know, and I don't know.

Throughout the celebration we talked and confabulated without words, and a pure loving relationship was built between us that was derived from our allegiance to the master of all believers, Ali son of Abu Talib, greetings to him.

My first visit to his village was after his death, and when I arrived there, his son Haj Hassan Khalaf passed me a rolled piece of paper containing a message from his father to me. When I opened the paper, I read the debate of the Abbasid ruler Al Mamoan on the superiority of Ali on all other companions of the prophet (peace be upon him and his family).

Sheikh Ali Khalaf's first meeting with our Sage

Prior to the Zionist invasion of Sinai; Sheikh Ali Khalaf used to connect to and attend a gathering/*majlis* for a Sheikh named Eid Jareer. Sheikh Eid Jareer was man with clairvoyance and Sheikh Ali Khalaf was fond of him.

On a *majlis*, Sheikh Ali was attending for Sheikh Eid a young man from the Nile Delta attended. The man had an evident dignity and was received by Sheikh Jareer and seated next to him. A cup of tea was served to the visiting man. He drank it and said, "The purpose has been fulfilled." The man requested dismissal from Sheikh Jareer to leave and return to Cairo. Sheikh Ali proposed to accompany the visitor to the taxi stop for his return to Cairo on a 6-hour journey.

After the visitor started his travels Sheikh Ali was confused by the visiting man. He didn't comment nor did he sit with Sheikh Jareer in private. Sheikh Jareer then told him about the young man that "This young man doesn't have a vein that beats for any other but Allah." This comment wouldn't have come from Sheikh Jareer for no reason.

This story made me love Sheikh Jareer although I never met him before. He moved to an village called 'Island of Saud,' west of the Suez Canal, during the invasion of Israel to

Sinai and he passed away there. A small shrine beside a mosque was built for him.

After my master passed away, I decided to conduct a tour to the shrines of all saints, Sheikhs, and brothers I had a relationship with. During a weekly Friday majlis conducted in Abu Al Ghait at the building of brother Haj Mohamed Shafiq, I discussed with a group of friends and brothers my plan including Sheikh Hassan Khalaf who did accompany me on most of my tour.

We started our tour from Tanta on Sunday with a final destination as Saud Island. When we arrived in Saud Island, we found the mosque where the shrine resided, but the shrine was locked. Sheikh Hassan took us to the house of the deceased and Sheikh Eid Jareer's son came to our reception promptly. We returned to the mosque and he opened the doors to the shrine for us and we prayed and sent our greetings to the deceased. We wanted to depart as soon as possible in order to reach Ismailia (a coastal city) before dark. However, the son of the deceased requested and insisted that we dine at their house and explained that he had seen a vision of his father in his sleep last Friday night (the same night we had planned our tour on). His father informed him that dear friends will come to visit him, and he is to greet them. We had a meal and then we asked for dismissal to leave and start our journey back. The son was full of glee as we departed his house.

These events might be taken by the mind in wonder, however, all of those who were on this trip were aware of the interventions of the unseen world and the connection of the deceased saints with this life.

The poor fellowship of love

The dust of loneliness is on their graves.

As-Sheikh Abd-Alraoaf Awadi

Sheikh Eid Jareer

I didn't get to know Sheikh Abd-Alraoaf during his lifetime although I had seen him on more than one occasion in the *majlis* Hall. We didn't interact and I didn't know about him until he passed away to the Lord's neighborhood. I was later informed by the '*ahbab*' our companionship about him. They explained that he was a Sheikh and he had disciples following him. When he met my master, he asked all his disciples to follow my master, he stopped preaching as a sage and became a disciple himself under my master's umbrella.

This reflects the purity of his good will. If a person's aim is to seek Allah's love and approval, then there will be no difference between a compliment or a slander. It is unfortunate that many of the righteous religious canon scholars focus on perfecting the worship appearance while being oblivious to the core of faith, and hence they accuse the mystics and the followers of the path of mysticism of neglecting the canon law while in reality they are only focusing more on their motives and their intentions and not neglecting the canon law of God. I would like to emphasize that I am referring to the honest followers of the path of love and mysticism and not those who claim; for many do claim but few are true. The utmost wonder is the love of the master of heavens Imam Hussain to his elder brother Imam Hassan as through history we learn that he didn't have any opinion nor a legislation throughout the life of his brother. We know for a fact that he was aware of his position and place from God as he was informed by his grandfather the beloved greatest prophet (peace be upon him and his family) and his father of highness Ali son of Abu Talib. From history, it appears as if Imam Hussain had melted and was consumed into his brother.

Let's return to Sheikh Awadi who I heard many stories about. One of the interesting stories I heard about him is of a time where he decided to travel for pilgrimage to Mecca with my master and the *ahbab*. When he took the bus to pilgrimage, he received news that his son passed away. He was shaken by the news, but he sent prayers for his son reverting back to the Lord through his words. He instructed his relatives to carry forward his funeral and all the required norms and customs, and he continued his pilgrimage trip to the heart of hearts, and light of lights, the Prophet Mohamed. Prophet Mohamed was instructed by Allah to call for pilgrimage for the people to came forth as pilgrims to him as God tells us in HAJ:27 "And proclaim to mankind the Hajj. They will come to you on foot…"

Reverting to our story, on our visit to Saud Island to visit Sheikh Jareer we had planned to pass by the grave of Sheikh Awadi on our way to Sheikh Jareer, hence, we took a longer route. During our trip my friend and brother Sheikh Hassan Khalaf was our guide and he took us to the graveyard where one of Sheikh Awadi's sons guided us to his grave. We recited few versus and sent our greeting to him and headed for a car to continue our trip where we met a lady. The lady passed a message to him telling him that her mother (Sheikh Awadi's widow) insists we visit their house. We wanted to continue our journey and we tried to get excused but with no success. They were insistent in their demand to visit them until we conceded and we accepted the invitation.

When we reached the house; the wife of Sheikh Awadi presented to us cups filled with a sweet juice and she told us of a vision she had yesterday in her dream. She said she saw her husband and my master greet a group of my master's followers and present to them a drink in extraordinary cups and she only identified Sheikh Hassan Khalaf in her dream (the only one she had met before). Her dream gave us happiness and joy for true is the word of our Lord where he says HUJURAT:7, "And know that among you there is the messenger of Allah. If he were to obey you in much of the matter, you would surely be in trouble. But Allah has endeared the Faith to you and has beautified it in your hearts and has made disbelief, wickedness and disobedience hateful to you. Such are they who are the rightly guided." (Mohsin)

This visit ended with our sweet drink at Sheikh Awadi's tomb after which we went to Saud Island where the tale continues as I have recounted in the paragraph above.

I Couldn't Sleep

"If Allah loved a slave, He will take him/her to heaven and will be pleased by the easy from him/her."

There is no doubt that the love Imam Baqir is referring to in this saying is not the love that is desired through intensive worship otherwise this will loop back (turn against the saying). A question is hence raised: How to acquire this love? The only anticipated answer is through devotion. It is the internal devotion and worship that can grant us this love. It can be in many forms such as desire and adoration, the clearance of heart from envy, trust in God, and the love and admiration to 'the love of God' Mohamed and his virtuous family. There is a lot of detail and depth in this understanding. However, we should highlight that we should aim to purify our hearts so that our few deeds are of greater value than a larger quantity of deeds in the Lord's balance.

Love lies in our hearts and our emotions rather than in our rituals. Rituals are a manifestation for the love and are means for reinforcing it in the heart. It is important to distinguish between the two and hence you will find that sages instruct their students to consistently watch over and purify their wills and motives and to seek the righteousness over their desires.

Listening is a mean for stressing and enforcing love in the heart. In some of my master's gathering he would say, "I feel an itch in my heart, O Sheikh Zaki, do itch our hearts for us?" Sheikh Zaki Al Sayyad was a Quran reciter, a oud player and a *munshid* (religious singer) who didn't have eyesight. He used to play on his oud and sing poetry that moved the heart with a beat for the prophet and his family. His tunes moved us, stirred our emotions, and reminded us of our yearn for the prophet and his family. The lyrics and melodies would drive us to devote to the light of the Lord.

Music has stirred controversy amongst Islamic scholars. Some scholars ban it and others permit it. My master used to say the righteous of it is good and the wicked of it is bad. Music and tune can be wind to your sail, music is the wind that will direct your sail. Your compass will determine your direction, and if it is to righteousness, then the wind will help you sail to it.

Sheikh Zaki was the main munshid consistent in his attendance to my master's gatherings. Few years prior to my master passing away, I had an interesting encounter with him.

During my stay in Oman, I used to miss attending the daily gatherings of my master. He used to hold a daily midnight gathering that his disciples and followers would attend. I requested from my master's grandson to arrange a daily video call where I could listen and watch the gatherings, I used to setup my PC and wait in my sitting room listening to tunes and religious music. During those days, I came across a song by Om Kolthoum called 'Aahl El Hawa.' In its lyrics, she sang:

"The lovers have left their beds, O night,
and they are gathered, O night,

in a company and I am amongst them."

I started to listen to this song every day before the broadcast would start. This was a private matter which I don't remember sharing with anyone.

On this year and on my visit to Egypt, I passed by the library in my master's building for a break. Sheikh Zaki was sitting there alone, I greeted him, and he replied. It was my first time to have a private chat with him and I took it as an opportunity.

He told me first about a vision in a dream he had seen where he was playing the Song 'Ahl Al Hawa' on his Oud and I was singing it in what he described as a beautiful sad voice.

During our conversation I enquired if he had an extraordinary experience with my master and he told me the following story as he said, "I have been attending the gatherings of our master for many years. I used to sometimes recite Quran or sing songs (religious Sufi songs and chants). The sayyid (referring to my master) had invited me to join him in his trip to southern Egypt.

"Upon our arrival the organizers were describing that the sayyid will be given a private room and me and the rest of the companions will share a wide room together and my bed will be placed near the door. I thought to myself that I should be treated like him and sleep in the other room; after all, I am a sheikh too. However, I did not share this feeling with anyone. The sayyid came to us and greeted us and told them to move my bed to his room and I was happy and praised the Lord that I will get to sleep in the other room. I couldn't sleep that night; whenever I closed my eyes, I would hear sounds of birds and animals in the surroundings, and I thought to myself why this sheikh is being approached by animals. On the next morning

I asked them to move my bed to the shared room; after all, I couldn't sleep on that night!"

Leave Your ICU Bed

One of our brothers from Egypt emigrated to Oman after facing difficulties in making a living in Egypt, upon his arrival he informed me that my master has had prepared an apartment for me in his building in Tanta (a village in Egypt, Nile Delta). I was overwhelmed with joy as I had an annual trip to Egypt where I would spend a month of my family's holidays in Tanta living heaven on earth beside my master.

I would like to point out here that the true joy and delight is in one's emotions rather than rituals, and in feelings rather than tangibles; for in morals is joy not in materials.

A poor man eating a loaf of barley bread might be living in joy, while a wealthy man sitting in front of a feast of dishes lives in misery and gloom.

We don't need to further explain this to our reader as we all in our experiences touch this when we see that there is no joy inherited from materialism while the joy in feelings is inseparable. If our reader insists in his/her perspective that joy is derived from materialism, then for the sake of argument we would say that the joy experienced by a wealthy man for a large sum of money he has saved in a bank is derived from the elation he gets from owning the money. This is evident in a child's behavior with a new toy where they cheer and get bored quickly; if the joy was in the toy itself, then joy should have lasted.

Our holy book Quran indeed draws a difference in vocabulary when referring to grace of living in luxury and true grace; this is observed through a movement on a letter on the word 'Nia'ma.'

And here we remember the versus of the mystical poet Sheikh Abu Hassan Ali Wafa as he said:

> My heart in peace, O' body, rest
> For in this delight I will live the rest
> My love's wings, I fall below
> Life is thus an easy flow
> My God's peace; under his bow
> No fear nor sorrow in his borough.

A more literal translation would be:

> O body, live for my heart's in peace
> This delight is everlasting
> I am under my love's patronage
> and who has his love's care, has an easy life
> Live under His banner, in God's peace
> No fear in His excellency.

Continuing our story on Egypt, knowing that my master had prepared an apartment in his building for me was great news. It could help us settle during our summer visits rather than staying at family friends, it would also ease our presence beside him and for accompanying him in his travels.

After that, and on one of my master's visits to Oman, he offered me to migrate with my family to Egypt. I knew then that the purpose of the apartment was for a permanent stay, not as a 'vacation house' during our visits. My children were filled with happiness and we made plans to travel by the end of the academic school year. We also made arrangements for our house to remain open for '*thikr*' gatherings (*Majalis* were private mass conducted in my house on a weekly basis as a weekly religious mass).

We looked at our traveling as a migration to God and his prophet, with hearts ruptured by the love of our Lord and His purified companions, Mohamed and his family. Our low-life (this life in Arabic is literally translated to low life as its always in comparison to the afterlife) and its qualities were short when compared to a day or a night beside my master where we would foster in his spiritual gardens and feast on the Lord's table where every nation can find its needs. He had the fruits of love and he had passion to the prophet's sanctified family and the water of life for those who seek God's mercy and the drink of piety for those with patience and pies of gratitude to those with needs and dessert of consolation for the poor (implies poor to God not poor as lacks wealth). Feasts that are filled with knowledge, science, love, devotion, plead, altruism and all that nurtures the human soul.

We prepared to travel; we packed our bags in our vehicle after taking his approval to drive to Egypt to keep our car along with us, we decided to start our journey on the afternoon of the 22nd of June after '*Thuhur,*' noon prayers. One of our family friends came to visit us on Wednesday evening (three days prior to our scheduled travel) wishing us a safe journey and expressing care and compassion.

My friend noticed me making a spontaneous motion repeatedly, he asked about it, and I shared with him that I was experiencing pain in my left arm extending to the left side of my chest. He told me that two of his brothers had similar symptoms and were diagnosed with clogged arteries and he insisted on taking me to the hospital, so I went along.

After checks by physicians, I was put under intense care and I was informed that I was to carry a cardiac catheterization.

My friend came on the next day and told me that he spoke to friends in Egypt and they mentioned my condition to my master and he sent me a message to leave the hospital under my responsibility, fly to Egypt, and he will send someone to bring the vehicle later; if there was a need for the procedure, it could be carried in Egypt. I called our Egyptian friend who had spoken to my friend who passed the message and he confirmed the content.

Then, I started planning to leave the hospital and signed a form declaring my own responsibility upon leaving the hospital; the hospital gave me some medications to take such as chewing pills and I went home. In the evening my master called, and he said, "O son, do you have the emotional capacity (self-readiness) for your planned journey to Egypt by car? I say an emotional (a self) readiness, not a physical one."

I replied, "Yes, my master, an emotional (oneself) readiness is present and praise to Allah."

He said, "Then pack your bags and come to us as you have planned and nothing shall harm you by Allah's permission."

I followed his instructions, packed my bags, loaded my car, and left by Allah's permission and his holy slave's blessing on Saturday noon, driving toward the 'direction of longing' and the 'ambition of lovers,' Taibah, the city of the love of Allah and his chosen one Mohammed (peace be upon him and his family). I didn't consume any of the prescriptions and medications provided by the hospital.

I traveled with my family to Al Madina and was honored by visiting our prophet and his daughter (Lady of all women) and the rest of the prophet's family, the sanctified kin, and those buried beside them, their loyal companions. Then I went to Mecca, followed by Jedda and took a ferry to Egypt from there and then settled in Egypt.

From the time I had arrived in Egypt, my master didn't mention my cardiac problem except once after a number of months on a visit to his physician, were he asked if I had any symptoms relating to a heart problem, or if I had a desire to see a doctor and I said I don't find a need.

I lived in Egypt a duration that God had in destiny for me to spend there, until came the time for me and my family to return to my home country. To Allah the praises and thanks from before and after for He is the most merciful.

From Where Did You Receive This?

One of the brothers and followers of my master used to live in a small coastal village between Muscat and Sur in Oman called Tiwi. A beautiful village with coastal lines carved by sea waves. It had a difficult gravel road connecting it to the main highway to Muscat previously. Today you will find a blacktop highway that makes the village well-connected, significantly improving its access when compared to the road conditions back in 1990s. I did visit the village when our brother Alaa used to live there. I remember seeing the waves carrying fish that can be seen from near the shore; a sight that had me thinking of this abundant grace provided for the people to eat from. I don't recall how I came to know Alaa but I do remember him and his family coming to stay in Muscat in my place for a night or two in many occasions as our relationship was formulated through our common attachment to my master and our love for the prophet and his family.

> There is an Arabic poem that reads:
> If you were with me in every state
> To carry my loads, I do not need.

There is no doubt that the Creator, Allah, is omnipotent. Muslims and believers of the Creator do believe in the Creator's power in principle and believe in the miracles performed by prophets told to us through our holy books. However, people find it difficult to believe in miracles that happen today or had occurred in recent days. People are skeptical to believe in a miracle that could happen today in the present.

Most religious scholars portray themselves as representatives of the religion as they learn the judicial aspects of religion, but they don't experience miracles in their lives. Learning religious law from *halal*, *haram*, what's permissible and what is not is indeed necessary and holy. However, it doesn't rise to, nor can it be compared to, the religious mysticism that grows the human soul and spirit. I do always focus on this aspect of faith as through it our beliefs grow for "the person who knows himself/herself comes to know his/her lord."

You will find that mystical leaders and scientists cherish and respect religious scholars as they comprehend the significance of religious law, but unfortunately this respect is not reciprocated by the scholars. Religious scholars identify themselves as those who have inherited the knowledge passed by the prophets and the family of Prophet Mohamed. Hence, they fail to understand mysticism, and in many cases, they attack those who practice it. I do excuse them if their motives were driven by a jealousy to protect the heritage of our prophet and his family. The problem and crisis arise when religious scholars attack mystical figures and when they consider them as defiled and unclean.

In reality, you will find that the knowledge and the inherited science from the prophets, the prophet and his family is large and great, and it is not limited to that recorded in the books on the judicial laws of religion. A quick review or read in the sayings and history of the prophet will find that judicial laws account for only a small share of the knowledge.

Reverting to our story; I was planning a trip to Egypt and Alaa came to know that I had intended to accompany our sage in his annual trip to southern Egypt in Shaaban. Alaa told me that if I was to visit southern Egypt, his father wanted to meet me. I was looking forward to meeting his father as well as he was an acquaintance of my master. His father came to visit me in the place of my sage's stay in southern Egypt. I was happy to meet him and he was telling me that our sage used to stay in his house in southern Egypt during his visits in the past. During our conversations he shared with me the following details.

During the reign of Jamal Abdul Nasser, Marxist ideologies started spreading amongst Egyptians. The marxism influenced many of the youth and had devastating effect on beliefs and faith of the villagers. He tells me that my master used to visit their village Sahara near Aswan (I might not be very certain on the village's name). My master used to preach and answer many questions and concerns that were arising on those days. On one occasion he was staying at Alaa's father's house. Alaa's father explained, "I took him to a room to rest in. He usually would wait for me to escort him out of the house and bring in food, but I forgot that he was in my home. He used to stay in a separate room that had its door landing directly in the common hall of the house. He used to remain in the room unless I came to his assistance. I forgot that evening, the next morning, and noon that he was in my house. I was startled as I remembered that my sage didn't leave his room and was not served any food and had been alone in his room for the duration. He must be furious, I thought. I went right away to the room and knocked on the door and went in. He smiled and passed me one of two plates that were in his room, the Lord only knows how he got them. I couldn't ask him the million questions I had in my head. Where did the good food come from? And who brought it to the room? I wanted to ask him from where did you receive this. But I couldn't."

It is indeed a pleasure and honor to serve saints of the Lord. Allah is Omnipotent and is in wealth from our service to his beloved slaves, and this story serves to remind us of this.

Prior to releasing this book, I did send this story to Alaa for proofreading and verifying that the details were accurate, and he has confirmed to me that the details are all as he had heard them from his father.

Weed Was Aspirin

I will be sharing below a very intriguing story that I have heard from my master directly. I am a little foggy on the details, but I remember the overall story and hope my master forgives me for any shortcoming.

My master shared this story during a conversation on the promotion of virtue and prevention of vice and ways used for reformation and education, it's a story about a fellowship from a small village under a sufism mystical banner in beloved Egypt. If I remember correctly, this story happened in the 1960s, where this fellowship held a '*thikr*' gathering in a small village nearby my master's hometown.

You might wonder why I refer to Egypt as 'beloved' although I am not Egyptian and nor my parents or my grandparents are Egyptians.

Egypt is a country with a long history of believers. They were the primary reason for the realm to return back to its legitimate path. They were the first to pledge loyalty to Imam Ali as he held the realm and they were then followed by '*sahabah*' (a term used to refer to whoever observed the prophet during his life) in Al Madina Al Munawarah. When Sayyida Zainab migrated to Egypt, masses left the cities barefoot to greet her as she was made to leave Al Madinah Al

Muwara. Yazeed, son of Muawiya, ordered his governor to make her leave the city out of fear of a public outburst after the tragic and devastating battle of Karbala. It is also the country that Imam Ali had written about in his testament to Mohamed son of Abu Bakar where he said, "And beware, Mohamed, that I have appointed you to my greatest soldiers to myself; people of Egypt" (Nahj Al Balagaha). Additionally; many conspiracies, massacres, and injustices occurred in Egypt for the purpose of distancing Egyptians from Ahlul el Bait (the Prophet and his family). Nevertheless, Egyptians are still committed to their love to Ahlulbait as they attend and celebrate *mawlids* and celebrations for Imam Hussain (the grandson of the prophet), Sayyida Zainab (the granddaughter of the prophet), Sayyida Nafeesa (a great granddaughter of the prophet), Imam Zain Al Abdeen (the great grandson of the prophet, and many other saints that descent from the Imams of Ahlulbait. I would like to mention here some of the popular names with popular shrines:

- As Sayyid Ahmed Al Hussaini Al Alawi Al Hashimi (commonly named: Al Sayyid Al Badawi)
- As Sayyid Ibrahim Al Qurashi (known by Al Dusuqqi)
- As Sayyid AbulRaheem Al Hussaini (known by Al Qinai)
- Abu Al Hassan Ali Al Hussaini Al Alawi Al Hashimi (known by Al Shathili)
  And many others.

Egypt remains to be loyal to Ahlulbait, although many satanic conspiracies have been made to diminish this loyalty.

Additionally, most Egyptian follow for their judicial laws, doctrines from Islamic scholars that are not descendants of the prophet and are not from Ahlulbait; such as Imam Al Shafie and Abu Haneefa Al Nauman.

Furthermore, Egypt remains to be one of few places in the world where the lineage and descent to Fatima Al Zahraa is still tracked and respected. There is official institute in Egypt that is concerned with tracking the genealogy of all those who are descendants of the prophet through his daughter.

Excuse my prolixity; reverting to our story about the gathering/*majlis* and its story, this gathering was conducted for the purpose of *thikr* ritual where attendants would repeat names and attributes of God as a mean of prayer. This *majlis* had an unprecedented situation where the attendants would prepare shisha and mix tobacco with Hashish and smoke it in their gathering while practicing their rituals and prayers, claiming that this allows them to be pure and focused in their devotion to God and help them get to spirituality. With their behavior, they violated God's orders and became consumed in their euphoric state of mind, ignoring the saying of our teacher (peace be upon him and his family) as he says, "What is intoxicant in large quantities, then a small amount of it is prohibited." They confused their joy of euphoria and their waste of mind from intoxication from Hashish with the trance of remembering Allah and emoting in his presence. And there is no power nor will but from Allah.

Between righteousness and falsehood, a feather, and between wickedness and piety, a person's will. Our will acts as a primary motive for our deeds and acts, not what we pronounce or say. A person who says when standing for prayer 'I am praying to be nearer to God' with an external reverence and care while looking after a public image and a positive propaganda, while the primary motive for the prayer is to fulfill what people have considered as the optimum manner for prayer and for seeking to Allah.

This is different from the person who attends gathering of *'thikr'* ritual to feel euphoria and psychological joy, and then his/her desire leads him/her. The desire will lead the person to use the *'thikr'* gathering as a mere cover through which the person's self will then regard prohibitions as *halal* (permitted deeds).

In contrary, there is a person who seeks a hardship in work to make a living and survive the pain of life while being consumed from within by Allah and his remembering and thus sees the suffering as an assist or an aid for submission to the almighty with a heart beating for the Lord and a clairvoyance that sees only Him. This person finds his rest hours as a release from burdens that hold him from total submission to Allah.

The person in the first state described has to continue his prayers with a continuous struggle toward a purer heart. Although his prayers as can be understood were of insincerity and for repute.

The second, which will be encouraged to remain active in being present in *thikr majlis* with an urge to rectify and repair the will and motives. This person should be disciplined from within until he/she practices *thikr* rituals with motives that will lead to the appropriate direction desired from these rituals. The acts he/she practices will not lead him/her to the direction desired from these *'thikr'* gatherings.

The third; his/her breaths are praises, his/her steps are prayers, his/her pain is a kept vigil, and his/her worship is a rise to Allah's kingdom, and his/her rest is a nearing to the Almighty.

If you confronted the first, you will break him/her and he/she might stop their prayer and you will be the mugger who stopped the slave in his/her path to the master.

If you exposed the second, in public or private, you have then removed his veil and softened his crime and potentially have closed the gates that could have led him to the Lord, so how would you respond to His master if He reproached you on it, had you intended virtue.

Hence, promotion of virtue and prevention of vice without wisdom can lead to catastrophic consequences or a bandit of the paths to God.

My master became aware of the conditions of these individuals and their gathering and their practices. He took upon himself to attend their gatherings frequently until they were used to him and his presence and they encouraged him to participate and lead in their rituals. When he was offered to smoke their shisha and Hashish, he refused and promised them to attend in the following week bringing along a better and purer drug compared to their 'commercial' product; he concealed amongst himself his intent to stop them from their addiction. He also promised them to take on all the costs of bringing the more expensive type of drug, taking the burden of the expense and using this as mean to spur their greed. He also explained to them that he will have to conceal the source of his purchase.

He came in the following week with white powder wrapped in paper rolls. He distributed it on their prepared shishas. He continued attending their gathering and promised them that he would keep on supplying them with this replacement. They liked what he supplied and they replaced their Hashish in their tobacco mix with the white drug he brought to them. He taught them the rituals of *thikr* and continued his attendance of their gatherings for more than a year until they got fully accustomed to using the white powder and never again desired their old hashish.

When my master became confident that they had stopped consuming hashish, he then abruptly stopped his supplies, but they begged for more and he refused. After their insistence, he told them of a pharmacy beside the shrine of Sayyid Al Badawi, its pharmacist knows him, and they can find their request.

They sent a smaller group to the pharmacy which they were able to locate. When requesting a 'special drug' from the pharmacist, he was outraged as he was honest in his sales and didn't sell any illegal drugs. The group then requested whatever my master used to buy, the pharmacist clarified that my master never bought any drugs, he simply took aspirin pills and grounded them to powder using a rock and placed it in paper rolls and handed it to them. They clarified from the pharmacist, "Was this what Sheikh An Nimr took?"

He replied, "Yes, this was his order every week."

They were stunned; they then took these paper rolls to their companions laughing and cheering, "Sheikh An Nimr has taken us to repentance, his weed was Aspirin."

This fellowship continued their regular gatherings after their repentance from the sin, and they were in glee and happiness to where the sage had taken them to. "Invite (people) to the way of your Lord with wisdom and good counsel."

Diabetic Coma

Praise to Allah, blessed and exalted be He. He has knowledge of the unseen and He opens the gates of knowledge to whoever He wants from his slaves. Some people are living between the human self and the materials; their bodies are living with us but their hearts are with God, they are living along with us by their humanity while their souls are floating in divine. The ignorant might see them as touched in their minds, while they have been touched by a great wisdom; it occupied them from what has occupied other people.

We had a house maid at home. She started living and working in my house since my early years of marriage. We treated her as a member of our family as her stay with us lasted for more than 20 years. She remained with us until she decided to return to her home in Sri Lanka. During her years working at our house, she would take decisions on household matters and argue with my children on some, but with shared love and respect.

It is difficult for me to refer to her as a servant for we considered her as family. However, to ensure clarity I am referring to her as our house maid (servant). After-all, we all are servants in one house; father, mother, brother, or sister, we all serve one another.

The maid used to respect and love my master and although his visits to our house in Oman would bring in more work and chores on her, with guests visiting day and night, she didn't complain of lack of sleep nor of additional workload. She used to find joy in his presence as we did.

On one of my master's visits to Oman she was off on her leave to Sri Lanka and she had departed to her country few days prior to his arrival. During the maid's vacation, my wife used to conduct the chores of the house alone and she had received a call from Sri Lanka from the maid's family informing us that she got severely ill and fainted and is currently in a coma in a hospital in Colombo and they are waiting for her disease to get diagnosed.

In a conversation between my wife and my master, she said to him, "Our maid left for her vacations and it seems she will not return as she has gotten ill and she is in a coma. We will have to look for a new maid." She asked him to pray for us to find a good maid to substitute her.

He replied, saying, "O daughter, she is in a diabetic coma and will recover soon and she will return to you by Allah's permissions."

My wife was surprised by the confidence in his reply. She didn't reply to him as she was astonished. She shared with me her conversation with our sage and how confidently he replied to her as if he had known about her illness all the way from Sri Lanka! I smiled to my wife and told her that we will wait and see.

After a few days from the incident, her family called us from Sri Lanka to give us an update and it was as my master had revealed. Her family explained that she had awakened from a diabetic coma, and her blood sugar level was balanced, and she was given medications to take and we came to know for the first time that she had diabetes. She returned to us as per her original schedule if I remember correctly.

She stayed in our house for years until she decided to return to her home country; she kept asking about my master and his children even after he passed away. We remained in touch with her for years after her final return to Sri Lanka until she passed away; may Allah overwhelm her with His mercy and blessings.

The Orphans' Painting

I had a childhood friend, we shared love and trust, he used to refer to me in his personal matters and he used to return to me in several of his issues and problems. His younger brother was emotionally unstable, and in their youth, he used to consistently worry for him. His younger brother respected me and would come to chat with me where I would teach him as an elder brother and provide him with counsel. He used to hold my respect and seldom he questioned me. As the days passed, my friend's brother stopped coming to me as he became more mature and older.

After years; he came to my place and started a conversation with me in a new preaching manner. He started advising me as if he was trying to project and reflect on my status. I was initially hurt but then I thought; he might have grown in his heart and 'wisdom is the believer's hunt,' so I decided to listen to what was of value in his conversation. In his talk, he started preaching me on the diseases of the heart from ego, pride etc. He had a logical argument and he was warning me to where I could fall to. As he left my house, I was in worry and fear as if the crackles of Hell where by my ear. I imagined that I had lost both this life and the afterlife. I was troubled from the devil's deception; I went out to the valleys and mountains crying to the lord and seeking his forgiveness. I felt misery that made me look like a *darwish* or a person who was mentally unstable. I imagine that had any of my acquaintances seen me in that state, they would have believed the rumors that had spread on me that I was a sufi mystical darwish, for my state would have been translated by the observer as if I am mentally ill or an 'attracted' sufi darwish. While I was in that state, I remembered that I should call my master immediately, so I drove back home and called him. Unexpectedly he answered the phone (usually his family members would receive his calls). As he answered, I started crying and he calmed me with the sweet tone of his words, I told him the conversation that ran between me and this fellow, and he then talked to me and then he recited on me the following verses "Surely, there has come to you, from your midst, a Messenger who feels it very hard on him if you face a hardship, who is very anxious for your welfare, and for the believers he is very kind, very merciful."

I might not have made it through the night if it was not for the calming words of my master, his sweet fatherly conversation. He who had the shining lights of his grandfather the great master Imam Ali (greetings to him) in him. It was indeed a long night through which I counted the minutes as they passed.

On the following day I went to work, and as I started my day a friend of mine gave me a painting covered with lite wrapping. He explained that this was a painting prepared by orphans of martyrs from south of Lebanon. As I removed the wrapping; there I read the same versus recited by my master written on it "Surely, there has come to you, from your midst, a Messenger who feels it very hard on him if you face a hardship, who is very anxious for your welfare, and for the believers he is very kind, very merciful." I knew then that this painting was from Allah's kindness and the care from being under my master's umbrella.

This young fellow ended his relationship with me completely, and I never heard from him again. I came also to know that he used to visit others and would provide them with ill-advice on me. I didn't pay attention to his acts and focused on what my master had told me and kept my self-reckoning with a plead to my grandmother Sayyida Zahraa and her daughter Zainab for their intercession and intermediary. This as I fortify myself from the major sins; for penance from the sinful actions is easy, while the sins of the heart will trap oneself in the devil's traps.

On the following visit of my master to Oman, as soon as he sat in the vehicle, he recited the same verses to me again. I understood it to be that he had sent the painting to me to be a gladdening. The understanding fell then on my heart that all of what had happened was from God's courtesy and the care of the righteous slave my master Sayyid Mohamed Ismail Al Laithy.

A Message from the Deceased

On a bright day during my stay in my brother and friend Mr. Mohamed Al Asali's house in an apartment he had built for me in his building in one of Cairo's suburbs where I stayed along with my family; we started a new day proceeded by a long night full of blessing of a gathering we had of prayer and singing (Inshad) mass of remembrance of the prophet and his family.

My friend Mohamed AlAsali had received a phone call from my master informing him that a friend of ours had passed away in Alexandria and we were to start traveling immediately from Cairo to Tanta to pick my master and head to Alexandria to attend the funeral and offer death prayers upon the deceased.

Our friend Haj Mohammed Al Safadi was a very decent and a well-behaved man, his wife and children shared his generous attitude. He used to run a business in the banana fruit market in Alexandria. He had infrequent visits to my master's gatherings, yet he considered himself a student of my master and one of his disciples. He used to invite my master to his house for an annual '*majlis*' gathering he would hold. It would include preaching, songs (*Inshad*), Quran reciting and other forms of religious prayers.

As I remember our friend, he had a common Muslim approach to religious knowledge and science as he didn't pay attention to details of Islamic laws and faith preaching, although he had a long history with my master and had attended multiple gatherings and masses conducted by my master. He however, had a strong love and attachment to my master and of course to our prophet and his family. He, like many believers, had faith that the prophet and his family's intercession would be his rescue in the afterlife; for the prophet's family are indeed Allah's true slaves.

It is important to note that the gatherings, masses or *majilis* we refer to within our text are generic gatherings my master used to conduct where Quran is recited, religious songs are prayed; they are more of feasts of spiritual guidance which includes a fruit from every basket; preaching, praying, and more.

When a person says 'me' or 'you,' he/she will not picture/intend a specified meaning for the words 'me' and 'you' in themselves, if you point onto a person's face, he/she will clarify it's 'my face' and not 'me.'

Similarly, if you pointed or directed toward another person's soul, he/she would say, that is my soul and not me.

We will not go through any philosophical explanations, but we are merely providing a hint that might help the reader grasp the content of the upcoming story. What a person means or intends when using the words 'me' and 'you' only interests us in the context of what a person might mean when using 'me' and 'you' while he/she is wearing the body in this life or while he/she is out of it in the afterlife.

Humans are created at least from the following elements:

- **Spirit**; which is the source of life to humans and we have a very limited understanding of what form it takes.
- **Human soul**; it has to do with human emotions and desires and the connection with the external world and our surroundings
- **Body**; which is a set of tools that the human soul utilizes to conduct its deeds.
- **Memory**; through it the person is presented as a distinct individual.

I have not mentioned the heart as one of the elements as its role remains to be mysterious. The complex ignorance in some lead them to limit the role of the heart to what modern natural sciences have reached to. They fail to see in their continuous development of theories and findings of new advances a sign of their ignorance and lack of knowledge. The case, however, is that the most knowledgeable scientists are those who see the vast knowledge they are yet to gain and currently lack. Those who realize more their ignorance are the ones with greater understanding.

The heart is merely one organ of the human body and regardless of the role it plays as a part it remains only one organ and our intention is not to explore the spiritual roles of body organs.

Parts or organs of the human body can get damaged and the person remains who he/she is, and the memory can fail but the person remains who he/she is, and the soul can be psychologically ill yet the person remains who he/she is; however, once the spirit leaves the body then all of that becomes as if it's not part of that same human.

The question is whether what remains from the human after the spirit leaves the body is the same person who was presented by the body in his material life; for sure this is the belief that all religions share.

And the remaining question is whether the spirit is the person known and presented to us during his life like an astronaut who is living through his costume in space and once he removes the costume; the costume is dead. Similarly; the human is present in a form that wears the body and once it leaves the body, the body is dead.

And if we accept and understand the above, then we will realize that the significance of our body is similar to that of the astronaut's costume; for he/she cares for his costume to preserve his body. This story will give you an insight on the other dimension.

Reverting to my story; as soon as I got the message with my master's instructions, we traveled by car – myself and my friend Mohamed – we picked up my master and his son Sayyid Tayib from Tanta and traveled to Alexandria.

My master didn't discuss anything about this trip through our journey and we reached to a specified mosque in Alexandria where the body of the deceased was prepared for funeral prayers and they were waiting for my master to arrive to recite. The family of the deceased had already arranged the ablution of the deceased body and its preparation and it was pending the funeral prayer.

When we arrived to the mosque where my master was expected to recite the funeral prayers, he pushed me and instructed me to lead the prayers and once I completed the prayer he said, "O son, be present at the burial and go down to his grave."

We left the mosque in a rush as the body was moved at a fast pace, and once we arrived, I was surprised by the burial arrangement.

There was a deep hole with long stairs leading to a chamber in the ground. There were horizontal holes dug on top of each other in the wall inside the chamber so that each body will be inserted in a hole with a series of holes on top of each other, so if you were on surface, there will be a number of bodies in separate holes on top of each other.

When the son of the deceased realized that I was present and sent by my master, he took me down the grave with them and they entered the body into the hole. I asked them to keep the body before closing it as I came to feel and realize that my master's instruction to be present for his burial was for me to indoctrinate the deceased.

Indoctrination is the act of speaking to the deceased with the main beliefs he/she should have, traditionally the following is included; Allah is our God, Mohamed His prophet and Ali is Mohamed's successor.

I did indoctrinate him with what I got from inner inspiration starting by informing him that I am my master's messenger.

I went back to my master and my friend Mohamed Al Asali, we took our vehicle and traveled back.

Our deceased friend Mohammed Al safadi had a son-in-law, his name is Abdul Majid. He and his wife were not in Alexandria during the burial morning and they arrived later on as they were staying in a small village far from Alexandria.

I received a call from Abdul Majid the following day and after passing my condolences and shared greetings, he asked, "What did you tell Mr. Mohammed Al Safadi at his tomb?"

I replied, "How did you come to know I spoke to him?"

He replied, "Sir, I have seen in my sleep a vision of Mr. Al Safadi where he said that you have passed to him a message from Sheikh an Nimr (my master) which was the reason for his survival... May I know what the message was?"

My answer to him was "Did he not say it was a message from the sayyid (referring to my master)?"

"Yes, he did say that," he confirmed.

Then I said, "Then alright... don't ask me for the content, ask the owner of the message."

Live your life like a person who has taken the shade of a tree in a long journey, and don't forget your stake from this life, your stake which will remain with you in your afterlife. And if you ask about the pleasures and joys, then these are left behind with the costume of the astronaut as they are left behind with your body. In reality, these pleasures are what life consumes and takes from you.

Furthermore, my master on one of his lectures, as I remember, had explained that the interpretation of the good deed in the verse 89 from Surat An Naml is the love of the Prophet Mohamed and his family and with this love no offense will be damaging.

Sheikh X

The story I am about to tell you shares a common theme in the experiences of our fellowship. Many of my master's followers had shared similar stories and experiences with me, but I was always busy with my sage than to get occupied with stories about him. Many have passed away and the details of their stories are not present to me today or have been vaguely remembered for me to share them with you, my reader. However, I hope the following stories will have your interest.

My brother Haj Mohamed Shafiq El Assaly tells me:

"I felt on a day a sudden urge to go and sit with our master. I traveled from Cairo to Tanta and I spent some time with our master in his library. My master then left the library heading up to his quarters. I then left the library and without thinking placed my hand in my pocket and, without counting, gave my master's son an envelope with money to pass to his father.

"Sayyid Tayyib took the envelope to his father and informed him that Mohamed Shafiq had given him the envelope to pass on to him. Our master didn't pick the envelope and asked his son to give it to Sheikh X who was sitting in the building's main hall on the ground floor.

"On his way down the stairs Sayyid Tayyib felt the envelope to be full of money, he counted the amount to be 480

Egyptian pounds. The amount seemed too high in Mister Tayyib's opinion, for our master usually gave Sheikh X a 100 Egyptian pounds periodically. Sayyid Tayyib headed back to his father who told him to give the envelope to sheikh X and that he had not requested from him to count the amount.

"On his way down Sayyid Tayyib met me and told me of what had happened with his father as I had not yet left the building and then he went to Sheikh X and passed the envelope to him. Sheikh X was relieved when receiving the amount.

"After a couple of days, I was sitting beside Haj Hassan Khalil and we had a chat and I told him about the incident. He then told me, "Two days ago, I was sitting in the hall when Sheikh X walked in with signs of sadness and worry. He wrote a paper to our sage explaining that he had borrowed 480 Egyptian pounds from the pharmacy for medication he had required for his wife. He expressed in his letter that he was shy to return to his county without the amount and he cannot explain to the pharmacist his state and he had decided to sit in the sage's hall until Allah solves his issue and he is able to pay back the pharmacist."

Here we can see that it's Allah's intention that Mohamed Shafiq would draw the exact amount Sheikh X needed without realizing, and for Sayyid Tayyib to take it to the master and then to Sheikh X without the need for counting or verification.

If you are under the heed
Sleep for all your worries will recede.

Some will say it's a coincidence and so says the blind. The sun rises brightly by chance and a moon reflects its rays by chance. The person with clairvoyance will see what those short-sighted will not; the intervention of the merciful hand from heaven.

In hearts of saints eyes that see
What normal eyes will fail to see
Along with reciting tongues
With words unheard by recording angels.

The Garbage Carrier

Abdulfattah 'Al Omda' was one of our dearest brothers within our group of followers of my sage. He was called 'Al Omda' as his father was a Sherif by inheritance, however, when his father died, Egypt changed the governance system of his village to follow the police under the state modern system and he didn't act as a sherif. He continued, however, to play part of the social role the sherif previously did and was known as the Omda for that. He asked me more than once to get our master's permission for him to visit Imam Ali's shrine in Najaf but alas the conditions didn't permit. He passed away after a long sickness may Allah bless his soul.

My master used to run an annual Mekkah pilgrimage trip for his companions to serve other pilgrims and for others to join as well and practice the Haj ritual. Many accompanied my master's trip; a group of his entourage and guests. On one of the years a building was rented fully by my master for his group in Mekkah, as the number of pilgrims accompanying him was high. The companions of my master sometimes fell short from serving all pilgrims' requirements.

Haj Abdulfattah told me that on a day before the morning prayer (before dawn) he saw my master climbing down the stairs after gathering all the garbage from the upper floors. Al

Omda was in tears at the sight and stopped my master short. Although my master slipped from him, he went again and insisted on taking from him the garbage. He said the he felt as if he was being pushed away by our master's status, but emotions made him insist on picking the garbage from our master's hand.

They then made sure all garbage was collected before people went to bed.

My Sage's Spouse

We have been storytelling of my master's companions and it is hence necessary that we remember his wife. My master's spouse was a woman who consumed her life in the service of the Lord through her consistent efforts in providing care and service to all gathering held by my master.

In the early nineteen nineties I used to go annually to Mecca and AlMadinah for pilgrimage with my master. The pilgrimage season fell on summer as the pilgrimage is dated on the lunar Islamic calendar. The heat in mecca was high with temperatures reaching to 50 degrees Celsius during the daytime. Water coolers were used for cooling tents and salt pills were distributed to pilgrims to prevent dehydration.

For pilgrimage, my master had a significant number of people joining him from Egypt, some of them where his affiliates and others who joined for pilgrimage only.

On one of the pilgrimage visits; my master's wife joined the trip. In Arafat, I decided to check the cooking arrangements to help and support the service, it is an honor to prepare food and drinks for pilgrims. I was surprised as I saw my master's wife standing by the large cooking pots and overseeing cooking of the food herself. She stood there with a smile and her big heart talking kindly to those helping around her. She was my master's wife and she would have been served by all the companions present yet she chose to help in the cooking. Families of preachers, sages, and leaders are usually inclined to pick a place where the service is easier or upfront, yet she chose to stand by the hot cooking pots in the summer heat of Mecca. Additionally, she was old in age yet she stood by the fire cooking when the tents where hot although they were cooled with ice water coolers. I was truly surprised by the scene, and I wonder if families of popular scholars and preachers with such number of followers would have stepped to conduct such a strenuous task; I doubt. She, however, worked with humility and glee. Her behaviors were only of kindness and care of a giving mother without any vanity.

I would like to reflect here a saying by our prophet where he told Imam Ali, "You came to this life to be inflicted not to inflict on others." I felt that the behavior was an extension to the behaviors of the prophet's family.

She spent her life in service and in strive with my master, supporting in every celebration of Ahlulbait. She was indeed an example of a truly selfless and sublime person. She passed away on the tenth of Muharram, the day where the deceased is honored in sharing their loss with the loss of the prophet's family.

My master once told us of a dishdasha that he had which had a hole in its pocket and he didn't know of. He had put in a small amount of money in the pocket and whenever he extended his hands into the pocket, he used to find money. His wife had once found the torn pocket and sew it without his knowledge. Since then the pocket wasn't the same again.

Al Qahhawi

The Prophet Mohamed stood by a graveyard in 'Qulaib' along with one of his companions and he started speaking to those in the graves, so his companion objected, "O messenger of Allah, you are calling the dead!"
And the prophet replied, correcting, "Your hearing is not better than theirs."

There is a thin barrier between the living and the dead. The living are in this life while the dead have left their bodies and moved on. The dead are dwelling in another dimension and after acknowledging their presence in another dimension; you cannot deny the ability to communicate with the dead. Only the person who claims having all of knowledge and science can say for a fact that there can't be any communication with the other dimension and such a claim is driven from ignorance. Ignorance is not an evidence for the ignorant.

Humans are made from clay; as believed by Muslims. Some of this clay was mixed with the clay of heaven. I would like to share with you the parable of the tourist. The tourist visited the house of a righteous man in the foreign lands. He observed that the house had no furniture, so he asked, "Where is the furniture of thine house?"

The righteous man replied, "What about thine furniture?"

The tourist exclaimed, "I am traveling and will return back to my home," and the righteous man replied, "And so am I." We are traveling between this life to the afterlife where we will dwell longer.

My master's companions told me that whenever my master would pass by the palm trees on the edges of a village on Cairo's suburbs called Qalaj he used to say, "O palm trees, under your shade lives a beloved person to me" and it appears to be that due to his strong love for this person who lived in Qalaj he used to encourage his companions to live there.

In Qalaj there was a man with no legs who lived in a small house along with his mentally ill brother. He took care of his brother and he worked on fixing watches from a small window from his home in an area where most of its residents were of low income. Placing two wooden sticks under his underarms, with a turbine on his head, he used to raise his body and drag himself to move small distances at a time. Putting this image in your head, you will have feelings of compassion and pity, but that would not have been the case if you had met him in person. You would have been taken aback by his majestic aura which along with his physical condition seemed to have been granted to him by the Lord in a unique mix.

This great man was Sheikh Ibrahim Al Qahawi, he was a follower of my master and he carried a weekly gathering which he led as per my master's instructions to him. His community referred to him for counsel and for resolving disputes and arguments amongst them. People were respectful of him and greeted him with reverence and stood for him out of respect. They took blessings from him, and he was to them a fulfiller of their needs.

A unique story that is told about this righteous Sheikh was during his encounter with an Egyptian military officer passing by him. He called upon him loudly in a provocative manner implying "Your seat is with me." The officer controlled his temper when he saw the caller to be an old handicapped man and he let him be. This brigadier explained that later on, he joined my master's group of followers and changed his place of residence to the same suburb where Shiekh Al Qahawi lived.

Shiekh Al Qahawi used to attend my master's gathering and he had an identified seat in the Arabic sitting arrangement (my master's venue had a main hall where he sat and most of the guests on chairs, and an extension to the left of my master's chair arranged in the form of an Arabic floor pillows and cushions seating). I held feelings of love and respect toward the Sheikh and he shared similar feelings back. Many who came to greet the sheikh would kiss his hands, but he never allowed me to kiss them. He used to kiss mine and when I used to withdraw my hands away with embarrassment, he would continue saying, "Pull your hands away if these hands are yours," [kissing hands is a common gesture in Egyptian culture used to show respect to significant sages and grandparents as well].

When the calling for the end to the period of ordeals came to Sheikh Al Qahhawi, and Allah permitted for him to leave this eternal body, he passed away and was buried in Al Qalaj cemetery. My master attended Sheikh Ibrahim's funeral when he passed away. He stayed at his grave kneeling on his staff. People departed the funeral, but my master remained until he and those who accompanied him remained behind. Before leaving the graveyard, he said, "I remained by the grave to be ascertain of his status and I saw him walking on his legs and feet before leaving."

Years later when I was a resident in Tanta I passed by his grave on a visit to Cairo and recited versus of Quran on the grave. On that evening, I walked in to my master's library where he greeted me with a smile and asked, "Where have you been this morning, my son, did you visit Sheikh Ibrahim al Qahawi?"

I replied saying, "Yes, my master," and he commented saying, "That is why I can see him happy and in glee today."

May Allah bless and be merciful on Sheikh Ibrahim. It had not crossed my mind to write on Sheikh Ibrahim, but this night as I went to bed I felt his presence and resumed my night by writing the story I had just shared with you, my dear reader.

May Allah accept my love to his saints and his beloveds, and primarily their master Mohamed the Prophet and his family, as they are of favor on all universe.

Do You Think That I Don't See?

One of my master's sons was out of his father's circle. My master was angry at him for his acts and he then became distant and didn't visit his father nor attended any of his gatherings. One day I saw him present in his father's building. I asked his brother Mr. Tayyib if my master had 'banished' him from his house or not and he replied that he neither kicked him out nor let him in and he had 'left the door just open,' using an Egyptian common proverb to express matters that were not closed but left slightly open.

I sat with him for a conversation along with another member of our fellowship. He requested that I help him reestablish his connection to his father. I expressed to him that we would only want from him to follow his father's wishes and we would then place him above us. I told him that through repentance he can revert back to his father. He confirmed to me that he intends only to return back as a member of his father's fellowship and act in a good manner.

I shared with my master the conversation I had with his son. He told me that he only asks from his son to follow Allah's orders and to leave his group of friends that he has been accompanying.

A meeting with my master along with three other members of our fellowship was arranged. He expressed to my master his regret on the past and his desire to return back. My master replied to him with a similar reply to me that he only wants from him to leave the bad group of friends he currently had. He replied, saying, "Sir, I have left this circle of friends a long time ago and I haven't seen them nor connected to them at all for some time now."

My master then looked at him with wrath and said, "Do you think that I am in this chamber and I don't see what you do? Have you not been with person x and person y in 'specific place' on 'specified day?' You talked to him about 'he mentioned two specific topics.' Do you think you can fool me?"

The son then became silent and my master left his apartment's hall and headed back to his bedroom ending the conversation.

The Migraine Is Gone

This story occurred to a dear friend and brother of mine and one of the closest companions in the fellowship of my master who is Haj Mohamed Shafiq Al Asaly. I have mentioned him in some other stories too. I do remember him going through this experience, but I am here sharing his description of the detail as below.

"I was inflicted with migraine for 10 years and I had suffered from its pain for many years. Praise be to Allah I had fully recovered from it and it had not returned to me again since then.

"On a day I met my sister by coincidence as she was leaving the physician. I asked her of her visit and she then informed me that she had started getting migraines. I had a lot of empathy for her, and I shared with her my experiences with it and how I used to control it.

"As I was sitting later that evening, I recalled what *darawesh* and some mystics say of people sharing or carrying the pain of others relieving them from it. I then prayed to Allah to pass the pain from my sister to me as I found that I had experienced it and I would be able to bare it more than her.

"A while later the migraine started.

"The next day I called my sister and I found that she had taken her medication last night and she felt that she was in full health now and I knew that Allah had answered my prayer, praise be to Him.

"The migraine kept increasing for two months consistently. It became unbearable. No medication was working to reduce the pain. On one morning the pain reached to an unbearable level and I called the Sayyid (our sage). He answered the phone which was unexpected as usually someone else would answer his phone. He advised me where to place my hand on my head and asked me to repeat words of a prayer and the pain was gone. I was relieved, I thanked and praised the Lord and I went out to work. By midday the migraine returned back and the pain kept on increasing. By dawn the pain was not bearable, I took the phone again and called him speaking in pain and with heat to reflect my misery, and I told him of my pain, he replied, 'Enough of it… it has reached to us.'

"And I felt something leaving my head and all my pain was gone. It felt as if his words 'Enough of it' were the remedy. Praise to all and thanks to Him, He is the omnipotent as I have not gotten the migraine pain since then."

Haj Abdulraoof Sharaf or the Pilgrimage

Abdulraoof Sharaf was a retired legal councilor who had worked for the Azhar Islamic institute in Egypt. After spending most of his life working for Al Azhar, in his retirement he became an imam for a small mosque in his neighborhood in Cairo.

"Is there any reward for goodness other than goodness?" (Rahman, 60)

People who praise their own acts to Allah and bring them as a grace from them are in misery. Whilst those who see poverty and shortcomings toward the grace of the Lord are in happiness and glee. There are two aspects to our lives; a materialistic life and a spiritual life. The first is the acts, movements, and rituals the person conducts, while the latter are the motives, emotions and similar elements. Many people live their lives in negligence; forgetting the required preparation required for meeting the Lord. Some do dedicate their lives to Allah's remembrance with shed tears. There are many levels in between and additionally there are many stances that occur to one-self, resulting in the person moving from one state to another.

Beware that the motive and will to reach to Allah praised be He is in itself a good deed and it might be from the most important "for acts are by their motives and for each person what is his/her motive." Allah praised be He guides and shows the path of success to every honest person in his/her intent to reach to Him. Scholars identify the person who is in negligence of his ignorance as a complex ignorant and it is perceived as an insult. I find that the complex ignorant will be judged based on his spiritual life not his materialistic life. Hence, the person with a good motive and intent will not be left behind but rather have a good return from Allah by His permissions.

I would like to mention here a word usually mentioned as being said by the prophet (Elohim, pray, greet, and bless him and his family): "A person from you would be acting with deeds of the dwellers of the heavens until there is an arm between the person and heaven but then the person is overcome with the booked and conducts the deeds of the dwellers of hell and then enters it," which Al Bukhari and Muslim have reported.

My sage and teacher Sayyed Mohamed Ismail Al Laithy had a clarification of sort to the prophet's saying. He used to explain that this quote is missing 'as it appears to the public' from it. So, the person would be acting good or bad deeds as perceived by others. In Quran, Allah Says, "óThe relenting taken by Allah upon himself is for those who do evil and ignorance, then repent shortly thereafter. So, Allah relents toward them. Allah is all knowing, all wiseó. The relenting is not for those who do the evil deeds, until when the time of death approaches one of them, he says, 'Now I repent,' nor for those who die while they are still disbelievers. For them we have prepared a painful punishment," (AN NISA: 17-18). The verses further clarifies that the intention of the prophet's saying is to refer to the weak and ignorant of Muslims that act in foul with weakness and a heart oriented toward Allah and a regret from the conducted act. To the public, these are wicked people with wicked deeds, but in reality, their hearts are oriented to the creator and there comes a time where they will follow the good deeds and will move from hell to heaven.

On the other hand, you could identify people as good based on their good deeds, while in reality, they are practicing hypocrisy or are in vanity as they perceive themselves above others.

The most evident example to us all is Satan who was a worshiper of God. However, he had hidden vanity and ego within his soul, and it was manifested out of him when Allah ordered him to kneel to Adam and he refused.

In the story of Satan, we find a very relevant example to our above explanation. Satan was initially a dedicated worshipper of Allah and was included in Allah's order to His angels. However, when he was ordered and tested by Allah to kneel to Adam, he defied Allah's order saying, "I am better than him, You created me from fire and You created him from soil." His failure to concede brought forth the arrogance and insolence that were within him. The prayers and worshipers of Satan appeared externally as the deeds of the dwellers of Heaven but not in their core.

So, to our Self, we say... beware... beware.

"There might be a good deed that inherits arrogance and pride that is worse than a bad deed that inherits lowliness and humility."

My master used to remind us regularly by saying, "The penitent awaits mercy while the person who is in admiration of himself awaits detestation," of the teachings of his grandfathers the imams of Muslims. Ali ibn Abi Taleb (Greetings to him) says, "A vice that is bad to you is better to Allah than a good deed that you like." Additionally it is mentioned in his proverbs in Nahj Al Balagha and also quoted from Imam Jaafar Al Sadiq, "A man commits a sin and then he is remorseful, and he then makes a good deed and that puts him in glee and so he loosens. It is better for him If he had remained in his earlier state than his new state."

I hence remind you and myself for our greatest enemy is the soul within us.

Reverting to Sheikh Abdulraoof who had spent his life in scholarship learning Islamic sciences; he was oblivious of two main pillars that believers should have; loyalty and assertion to Allah's Saints (Al-Wilaya) and the renouncement and repudiation of their enemies. There is no doubt to us that showing assertion and loyalty to the saints of Allah, primarily Ahlul Kissa'a and Imams of Ahlulbait who Allah appointed as saints, is an essential pillar of a person's belief. As a matter of fact, this applies to all appointed imams and saints by Allah. The disagreement can be in the identification of these individuals.

The sheikh came to know of my master in the house of the son of his cousin in a suburb of Cairo. At the end of a weekly gathering as Sheikh Abdulraoof was about to leave the room my master called on him, "Have you been to pilgrimage to Mecca?" he asked.

Abdulraoof replied, "Not yet, Master, I didn't get the opportunity yet."

My master then said, "Make your plans that you will go to pilgrimage with us this year and pass your passport and documents to your nephew Haj Mohamed so he can prepare your visa."

Shiekh Abdulraoof replied to the sage with a polite 'yes, sir' and then headed to his cousin's son Haj Mohamed telling him, "Son, I don't have any money for the trip nor for even issuing a passport." An honest man he was, indeed, for he worked in Al Azhar for long years yet he didn't have any money saved. If you had looked at him, you would have only seen a decent man with no signs of poverty. He reminds us of Quranic verses, "An ignorant person takes them as free of need because of their abstinence. You know them by their appearance, they do not beg people importunately, and whatever good thing you spend, Allah is all All-Aware of it," (AL BAQARA: 273).

Haj Mohamed replied to him, "Don't worry, Uncle, for our master has invited you and he will support this, consider this trip an invitation from him and on his expense."

Annually, my master had a Mecca pilgrimage trip where the fellowship would prepare all the travel arrangements required for the trip and pilgrimage. On that specific year the cost of a pilgrimage visa spiked in Egypt and was sold in the black market mainly at a very elevated rate. Haj Mohamed spoke to me about the situation. I shared this news with Sheikh Hassan Al Farsi in Oman, and he proposed that a number of visas get arranged through a friend who works in the Saudi Embassy in Muscat. The plan was to bring a group of 20 individuals from Egypt to Oman where the Saudi Embassy in Muscat will issue a visa for Haj to them. We managed to secure 14 tourist visas to Oman and our master instructed the Haj Abdulraoof be one of the fourteen people to come to Oman.

The group arrived in Muscat but there was a delay from the Saudi Embassy in Muscat. The embassy was waiting for an approval from Riyadh. On the second day of Thul Hijah; eight individuals from the group became upset. They came to believe that our plan was to fool them from the beginning although we were transparent with them throughout the process and they decided to leave back to Cairo.

The remaining group of six were all friends and they only had respect and gratitude to my sage. I had four of the six living in a hotel while my wife and I invited a couple to stay in our house as guests as they were family friends. The 4th of Thul Hija was the last day on which pilgrims are allowed to enter Saudi Arabia for pilgrimage and upto the 6th of Thul hijah we had not heard back from the Embassy. The couple living with us decided to return back to Cairo. They felt that they had passed the last day for entering Saudi already and they could spend Eid back home. He requested that we buy him the earliest available ticket to Cairo if possible. While we were seated in my reception room, he took a nap. In his sleep he had a vision as he saw that he was in a great mosque in a group prayer and the Imam of the prayer was dressed in as Shia sheikhs dress. He called on the hall, "Who wants to go for Haj?" He replied in his dream, "We do, Sheikh." The sheikh replied to him, "Bring me your passports," and he replied, "But the day for entering Mecca has passed?" The sheikh answered him, "Give me the passports and leave the rest to us."

We were all happy by his vision and his wife felt that this was Allah's message that by their motive they have been considered amongst the pilgrims. They insisted to leave for Cairo and so Haj Hamdi and his wife left on the morning of the 7th of Thul Hijah to Cairo. I left the airport and my mind was turning. *What should we do with the rest of the group?* Haj Mohamed was worried as well. His uncle Haj Abdulroaoof was amongst the four remaining individuals waiting for the visa. He was expecting to attend Haj given that this trip was a recommendation from the sage. If the circumstances led to him not traveling, this could influence the perception of his uncle.

I drove out of the airport into the highway and my mind was racing. As I was lost in my thoughts, my phone rang and it was the Saudi Embassy. The caller confirmed I was Haider and told me of 20 visas approved now from Riyadh for Haj and I could take the passports for whoever I wanted, to get stamped with Haj visas. I was astonished as I didn't expect the visas to be issued after airports closure to Haj pilgrims. I called the remaining pilgrims and shared with them the jolly news. I asked them to pack their bags as I would go to stamp the passports. I was concerned with finding tickets to Jeddah. Airlines were fully booked on these days. As I called airlines, my fears were confirmed that not only seats were fully occupied, waiting lists were blocked too.

I then called a family friend who worked for an airline and held a senior position. He sympathized and told me that he would get back to me. At 10 am he called and told me of 4 tickets available for a flight departing at 1:30 pm and I was to take the passengers to the airport by 12 at noon. I drove to the embassy, stamped the passports and headed to the hotel to pick up the pilgrims. They were in happiness and glee as they were pronouncing their prayers of thanks and gratitude to

Allah and I can still recall their calls of "Allah is Greater," "Gratitude from our master Hussain," "Gratitude from Zainab daughter of Ali."

We were running late but we managed to arrive right before counters closing. The check-in staff asked for their visas, I told him they had pilgrimage visas. He expressed his surprise given that a few days had passed to accepting pilgrimage visa holders. He consulted with his superiors after confirming the date the visa was issued on and they allowed them in.

I then called Haj Mohamed to fly into Muscat on the same day and fly to Jeddah with me on the following day so we could accompany our master and serve the pilgrims and he did. He booked a business class ticket and arrived on the same evening in Muscat. On the next morning we got him a visa from the Saudi Embassy, and we headed to the airport. The check-in staff as well said that Jeddah airport stopped accepting pilgrimage visa holders. Similarly, I told him that the visa was stamped on the morning. He then went to his superior and they were talking and then they started laughing. He told me, "We had a similar situation yesterday. Four passengers came with visas signed by the Saudi Embassy, they were allowed into Jeddah, but the airline was fined. We had to pay fifty thousand Saudi riyals per passenger as a fine from Jeddah and we were asked not to repeat this mistake again. We can't allow him to fly but you as a GCC citizen can fly to Jeddah, no problem." Haj Mohamed Al Asali insisted that I fly to Mecca and that he will fly back to Cairo so I could be with our master. He was saddened that he couldn't join us but was happy to observe the support from the Lord and His mercy. Such a plan makes us touch the providence and care of the Lord. Haj Mohamed told me that he had no doubt that they would conduct pilgrimage as our master had directly invited Haj Abdulraoof to attend and he believed that the promise of my master would come true.

On the pilgrimage trip my master in Menna asked me to lead the prayer of the companions. As we were sitting in the camp, I felt within my heart that he would be asking me to lead the prayer so I concealed myself on a corner. He called "Where is Mr. Haider?" I didn't reply from all the shyness in myself but he called again, "Where is Mr. Haider?" And the companions loudly called on me to answer him. He then made me lead the prayer and as I was praying, I forgot whether to pray a full 4 kneels or pray a traveler 2 kneels prayers. I asked him in my heart to answer me but I didn't hear an answer and I prayed a 4 kneels prayer. After I finished he said, "The only person who prayed a 4 kneels prayer was Uthman bin Afan as he claimed all the lands of Muslims were his." I was told that he said more than once during the prayer that in Menna the prayer is 2 kneels only. However, my prayer leadership within his presence had me occupied from listening.

We completed our pilgrimage and we all went back to our home countries. Haj Abdulraoof went home a new man and started his short life after his pilgrimage by writing poetry for the eulogy of the prophet and his Ahlulbait. He wrote fourteen of them and he called them Flower 1 to Flower 14. He shared them with me and read them to our master in Egypt.

Mr. Hamid and the Infliction of Marsafa

One of the most loyal followers and companions of my master was Haj Hamid. He was a loyal follower, he served in all events, sermons, and ceremonies held by my master. He had a pure heart and I knew him for years. He used to pray silently in the mosque at my master's venue after the departure of all others, and he would give his opinion in arguments with a smile and leave quietly. My master used to call him the hidden saint.

There is a popular hadeeth, a saying by the Prophet Mohamed which is very popular amongst Muslims and is accepted by many, were he says, "Jews became divided into seventy-one sects, Christians became divided into seventy-two sects and my nation will be divided into seventy-three sects, all of them in hell except for one." The context of the saying is present in various books and they all share the content that the Muslims will be divided into sects and only one sect will survive hell.

In order to understand and translate the meaning of this saying; many of the Muslim scholars explain this saying by interpreting the 'surviving sect' from the 73 sects being more related to those with good deeds and a clean heart to the Lord.

However, we understand the meaning of this saying by reverting back to Imam Ali (the gate to the prophet's knowledge) who explains it in reply to a question which said, "O prince of believers, how is a person who did not believe in your imama (inheritance of the religion) and did not hold enmity against you, and did not hold rivet nor was loyal to you nor disowned your enemy and said 'I don't know' with honesty?" The imam replied, "Those are not from the seventy-three sects. The prophet intended by the seventy-three sects the ones with intention and stance, the sects are those who publicize to themselves and call for their religion. One sect only follows the religion of the merciful and seventy-two follow the religion of the devil; they give approval to those who accept their faith, and vindicate themselves from those who disagree with their faith. However, those who have believed in Allah as One and believed in his Prophet Mohamed, and they did not know of the requirement of our loyalty nor did they know of the aberrance of our enemy, and they did not constitute, and did not introduce *harams* and *halas* (add or remove from faith and doctrine of religion) and they followed all what the Islamic nation doesn't have a disagreement on from Allah's orders, sanctified and exalted He be, and remained out of the dispute of the arguing parties from the nation, and they did not constitute, nor did modify a *Halal* or a *haram* and they don't know what has come (from teachings/guidance) that would otherwise show what has been problematic with them, then they will survive."

We understand from this explanation by Imam Ali that the prophet did not intend that most of the Islamic nation will fail to survive but rather that those with independent banners, calling for a doctrine and modifying the religion of the Lord will fail to survive. My master, hence, had a name or a title which he used for his fellowship; "Lovers of Mohamed-like Purity" to unite everyone under.

My master shared with us how he came to use this title on all his gatherings and writings. My master was running a service to feed visitors to the celebration of Imam Hussain's Mawlid in Cairo; his companions were in disagreement. They came from various sufi/mystical affiliations and each group wanted to post the name of their affiliation on the service. My master explains that he was saddened by the breach amongst a group of believers. He says that on the same night he saw a vision of Sayyida Fatimah Al Zahraa the daughter of Prophet Mohammed as she handed him a poster written on it "Lovers of Mohamed-like Purity" (احباب الصفاء المحمدي), he then shared the news to his group and they all took this as glad tidings and they modified all the banners to reflect the new title. He continued to use this title on all his activities and services he conducted in Egypt.

In the holy Quran we read, "Surely, those who have made divisions in their religion and turned into factions, you have nothing to do with them," (Translation of AL ANAAM 159 Taqi Usmani). For Allah, blessed be He, abhors every speech or attempt that divides Muslims and inherits hatred and grudges amongst them.

In the early nineteen sixties my master was approached by a group of people from Mirsafah for support; Haj Hamid's village. A major distortion had occurred in their village by a group. They were preaching people and forcing their leadership upon the village. The village Mirsafah is near to Banha (a metropolitan city) and my master addressed them through a letter which had an impact upon the villagers and the ordeal passed. If you read the letter with care, you will find that it is a constitution to be followed by preachers and scholars. Below is the context of the letter:

My Sage's Letter

By the name of Allah most Merciful and most Beneficent

And praise be to Allah and greetings upon the servants those He had chosen for Himself.

"Who can be better in words than the one who calls towards Allah and acts righteously and says I am one of those who submit themselves."

To respected scholars and to those who care about the condition of Muslims in Mirsafa specifically and the rest of the world, Allah's greetings upon you and his mercy and blessings.

One of the main duties required from Islamic scholars and preachers that they shall purify their wills and tongues from what inherits failure and defeat amongst Muslims and what causes weakness in their ranks. They shall keep their souls from mistrust and conjecture while fearing Allah in what they say and they shall refer to the trusted resources for their preachment. They shall avoid triggering fanaticism and prejudice that can rupture the nation's body and can lead to the groups parting by causing ignorance that provokes aversion and conflict leading to acts that the mind and judicial Islamic law both do not permit. They are required to follow a manner that was followed by the prophets in their preaching and arguments as explained by God in his holy book, "Do not debate with the people of the book unless it is in the best manner," and praises be to Him as He says, "Invite to the way of good with wisdom and good counsel. And argue with them in the best of manners," and Exalted be He says, "Repel with what is best and you will see that the one you had mutual enmity will turn as if he was a close friend."

And exalted and sanctified be He says in the story of Hud, the prophet, "Said the chiefs of his people who disbelieved: indeed we see you in folly and we believe you are one of the liars," and the prophet replied to them saying, "He said: O my people there is no folly in me but I am a messenger from the Lord of all the worlds," and Allah has ordered the Prophet Mohamed to tell the infidels "And we or you are either on the right paths or in open error."

The prophet did not refer to them as being in deception and error without doubt or uncertainty, although the infidels are in open error with no doubt nor any hesitation.

Hence, the shortest paths to take people to the path of God is through following the manner He described in preachment to argue with the best of manners; the better manner... and the most complete approach is the one the Lord has ordered his prophets to follow for delivering his messages.

Therefore, we should be following the preachment approach that is far from mistakes and sanctified from cursing while acting with leniency and gentleness.

The preachment conducted should be based on knowledge and science with a consideration for the beliefs of other Muslims as being based on correct basis if possible while avoiding any presumptions, any personal inclinations, and any wicked fanaticism.

Allah says in His holy book, "And do not follow a thing about which you have no knowledge. Surely the ear, the eye and the heart – each one shall be interrogated about," and He says, "So it is through mercy from Allah that you are gentle to them. Had you been rough and hard-hearted they would have dispersed from around you."

And Allah tells us in the Quran about Hud the prophet, where his people replied to him saying, "And we believe you are from the liars." The verse infers that Hud's nation did watch their manners as they did not say in certain that he is a liar as per the verse. How can a believer of Allah who should be behaving in Allah's manners be judgmental on other believers accusing them of infidelity or of being sinful? What excuse this person will bring to the Lord on why accusing a Muslim of infidelity or why cursing and swearing was used in arguments which could raise grudges that will not allow the truth to be revealed and for the reality to come forth. The honest scholar would not permit for himself to refrain from using the behavior the Lord has mandated. We seek refuge to Allah if in-between the workers and scholars a person whose weapon of argument is only cursing and prejudice and the speech without knowledge or by contradicting facts as if they have not heard the words of the God as He says, "It is the disbelievers in Allah's verses who forges lies and it is they who are the liars," and we seek refuge from whoever prefers or weighs up his doctrine's characteristics over the Islamic character and hence they reduce the latter by supporting the earlier.

I present this and I am willing to discuss with you in whichever manner you prefer and in any place you would like to remove doubts and to provide counsel for Allah, his prophet, the imams of Muslims and for the public.

And peace be upon you and Allah's mercy and His blessings.

Praises to your Lord, the Lord of pride from their descriptions, and greetings upon the messengers and thanks and praises to Allah the Lord of all the world. And Elohim pray upon the best of your creation our master Mohamed and upon his pure and gracious family.

Drink from Me (Poem)

Put my heart to the test
You will find my honest woe
For inside my love nest
You'll only find me in low
My liking of the sun
Has put my tears in flow.

Lo, for it put in flames
My heart's inner blood
And my eyes are in vain
As its lights are a flood
But in my sight I have gained
Through what now hast shut.

Do not tell me; how are you being
As I rover in my baffle
Do come to me, as I am flowing
You will find my drink quenching.

My fellow, don't be vain
Come and drink my ale.

About Him

This is information about my sage:

His Name:
Mohamed Ismail Al Laithy
His Byname:
Sheikh Nimr
His Genealogy:
He is a descendant of the Prophet Mohamed through a lineage that is through Imam Moosa Al Khathim.
His Birthday:
Wednesday, 14th of Jumada Al Akhir 1347 corresponding to the 24th April 1929
His Day of Descent:
Monday morning on the 13 of Jumada Al Akhir 1424 corresponding to 11th of August 2003
His Hometown:
Kafr Arshoof; a village in Tala in the State of Monofiyah in Egypt
His Residence:
Tanta, Egypt
His Shrine:
In his hometown in Kafr Arshoom in Egypt

His Children:

Two Sons and a Daughter

His Poetry:

He used to recite and distribute them without labeling them as his. Hence, there are many he distributed but cannot be confirmed as his. Two of his popular poems are for Sayyida Zainab and Imam Hussain but he has many others.

His Motto:

If you find a sweeter source than ours then go for it.

CPSIA information can be obtained
at www.ICGtesting.com
Printed in the USA
BVHW031424270622
640731BV00012B/258